Zac Efron

by Sheila Griffin Llanas

www.raintreepublishers.co.uk
Visit our website to find out
more information about
Raintree books.

To order:
☎ Phone 0845 6044371
📠 Fax +44 (0) 1865 312263
💻 Email myorders@raintreepublishers.co.uk

Customers from outside the UK please telephone +44 1865 312262

Raintree is an imprint of Capstone Global Library Limited, a company incorporated in England and Wales having its registered office at 7 Pilgrim Street, London, EC4V 6LB – Registered company number: 6695582

Text © Capstone Press 2010
First published in paperback in the United Kingdom by Capstone Global Library in 2012
The moral rights of the proprietor have been asserted.

Editors: Megan Peterson and John-Paul Wilkins
Designer: Joanna Hinton-Malivoire
Media Researchers: Marcie Spence and Tracy Cummins
Production Specialist: Eirian Griffiths
Originated by Capstone Global Library Ltd
Printed and bound in China by Leo Paper Products Ltd

ISBN 978 1 406 22953 0 (paperback)
15 14 13 12 11
10 9 8 7 6 5 4 3 2 1

British Library Cataloguing in Publication Data
Llanas, Sheila Griffin, 1958-
Zac Efron. – (Star biographies)
791.4'3'028'092-dc22
A full catalogue record for this book is available from the British Library.

Acknowledgements
AP Images/Matt Sayles, 23; Getty Images Inc./Dave Hogan, 21; Getty Images/Frazer Harrison, 11; Getty Images/Jeff Kravitz, 29; Getty Images/Jon Furniss/WireImage, 7; Getty Images/Kevork Djansezian, 5; Getty Images/Mike Flokis, 28; Newscom, 9; Newscom/Jeffrey Thurnher/The WB, 16; Newscom/PacificCoastNews, 9; Newscom/SHNS photo courtesy New Line Cinema, 24; Newscom/Splash News and Pictures, 12, 27; Rex Features/Startraks Photo, cover; Supplied by Capital Pictures, 15; The Disney Channel/The Kobal Collection, 17, 18; The Disney Channel/The Kobal Collection/Larkey, Adam, 6.

We would like to thank Isabel Thomas for her invaluable help in the preparation of this book.

Some words appear in bold, **like this**. They are explained at the bottom of the page, or in the glossary.

Contents

CHAPTER 1

Zac's biggest audition

It's 2005, and Zac Efron is handed a script for a new TV film. The 17-year-old actor likes what he reads. His **agent** tells him that Disney producers are looking for new faces to star in *High School Musical*. Zac really wants the lead role of Troy Bolton, a **high school** athlete who secretly wants to act. Hundreds of other young actors also want the part. Zac had performed in stage musicals and appeared in TV shows. He had even starred in two small films. He hopes his experience is enough to give him the edge.

At the **audition**, the hopeful actors have to act, sing, dance, and even play basketball. For his solo, Zac sings Mario's "Let Me Love You". The casting team like what they hear. They ask Zac to read through part of the script with Vanessa Hudgens, who is trying out for the female lead. Zac and Vanessa have good chemistry. The judges keep them together for the rest of the audition.

agent someone who helps actors find work

audition a performance by an actor who is trying out for a part

Zac starred on TV and in two small films before his *High School Musical* audition.

One by one, actors feel a tap on their shoulder and are asked to leave the **audition**. Zac braces himself for the shoulder tap, but it never comes. Finally, just one actor stands between Zac and his dream role. Producers send the boys home and tell them to wait for a phone call. Ten days later, Zac's phone rings. He wins the part of Troy! He doesn't know it at yet, but 'Zac Efron' is about to become a household name.

The only thing that separates me from 200 brown-haired, blue-eyed guys in LA is one single audition. I'll never forget that."

Zac from an interview with *Time* magazine

Zac and *High School Musical* co-star Vanessa were paired up at their second audition.

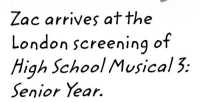

Zac arrives at the London screening of *High School Musical 3: Senior Year.*

Star Facts

Full name:
Zachary David Alexander Efron

Date of birth:
18 October 1987

Nicknames: Hollywood, Zaquisha, Zefron

Pets: Puppy, an Australian shepherd dog; Simon, a Siamese cat

Hobbies: mending old cars; working out

Party trick: "I can blow bubbles with my spit"; good juggler

Trademark: dimples

Idols: Johnny Depp; Leonardo DiCaprio, who is also his good friend

Likes: comic books; baseball; comedy duo Flight of The Conchords

Worst habit: scratching his skin when it gets dry

Treasures: his collection of signed baseballs; his Gibson guitar

CHAPTER 2

Younger years

Zac was born in San Luis Obispo, California, in the United States. His parents, David and Starla, met at a power station where they both worked. Their second son, Dylan, was born four years after Zac. The Efrons raised their sons in the small coastal town of Arroyo Grande.

Top of the class

Education was important in the Efron household. Zac had to finish his homework before he could chill out. But he didn't mind his parents' strict rules on getting good marks. Zac studied hard and earned straight A-grades. His favourite subject was English.

Zac relaxed by playing video games and skateboarding. He also went to watch baseball games with his brother and their dad. They turned up early to watch the players practise. Zac loved playing baseball and basketball himself. But to his disappointment, he was not a star athlete. Zac jokes that he still has nightmares about the time he lost a basketball match by passing the ball to the wrong team!

Zac, shown here at the age of 13, attended Arroyo Grande High School in California. He worked hard, but admits that he was also the class clown, telling jokes and making people laugh.

Star talents

Zac knew he would never be a professional athlete, but he had other talents. Zac could listen to a song on the radio and sing it back in perfect pitch. He often made up his own songs. He watched musicals like *Grease* and *Singin' in the Rain*, and acted out his favourite parts. Zac's parents noticed his talent for performing. They signed him up for singing and piano lessons. They helped to guide him towards the stage.

At age 11, Zac **auditioned** for a role in the play *Gypsy*. He won the part. *Gypsy* ran for 90 performances at the Pacific Conservatory of Performing Arts theatre in California. Zac soon became hooked on acting. He enjoyed making people laugh and hearing the applause. He got parts in other plays, such as *Peter Pan* and *Little Shop of Horrors*. Zac impressed the drama teacher at his school, and she helped him to find an **agent**.

"My dad convinced me to go out and audition for my first play. I went kicking and screaming, but little did I know my dad had just showed me the coolest thing on earth."

Zac, from an interview with Scholastic News Online

Zac, shown here at the age of 16, was a natural at stage acting.

Zac lived at home with his parents in Arroyo Grande, California, until he was 19.

Growing pains

Zac's mum began driving him to Los Angeles for TV and film **auditions**. Each audition meant a six-hour round trip. Zac was used to peforming on stage, where he had to **project** his voice. This is not necessary on TV. At his first big audition, Zac shouted his lines when he was supposed to speak softly. He blew the audition. Because of his inexperience, Zac was rejected from many other auditions.

Zac began to wonder if the auditions were worth his time. His mum was tired of the long days spent in the car. Zac was also missing school. To keep up his good grades, he studied overtime. He even posted homework to his teachers. But Zac enjoyed acting too much to quit.

"I wore goofy hats to school and did musical theatre. Most people thought I was a dork. But if you have a sense of humour about it, no one can bring you down."

Zac, on coping with teasing at school

project to make your voice carry far

CHAPTER 3

A rising TV star

In 2002, Zac made a small guest appearance on the US TV show *Firefly*. Appearances on *ER* and *The Guardian* soon followed. In 2004, Zac got his big break. He won the part of Cameron Bale in the TV drama *Summerland*. His parents rewarded him by buying him a wetsuit and surfboard for Christmas! At first, Zac made small guest appearances on *Summerland*. The show's writers liked his work. They developed the part, and Zac became a regular cast member.

While working on *Summerland*, Zac took on another tough role. He played a boy with **autism** in the made-for-TV film *Miracle Run* (*The Unexpected Journey*). The film was about a single mother raising autistic twins. Zac played Steven, the twin who wants to be a runner. Critics said his performance had depth and heart. Zac was thrilled to be nominated for a Young Artist Award for Best Supporting Actor.

autism a condition that causes people to have trouble communicating and forming relationships with others

Zac played an autistic runner in the TV film *Miracle Run*.

Riding high

Summerland was cancelled in 2005, but Zac's disappointment didn't last long. Later that year he played a jockey in the drama *The Derby Stallion*. Zac had to learn how to ride a horse for the role.

Zac (back row, second from left) joined the cast of *Summerland* in 2004.

After just three lessons, Zac could get his horse to do jumps and sprints. Zac did his own riding in most of the horseback scenes. *The Derby Stallion* did not show in cinemas, but Zac's film-making experience and hard work were about to pay off.

High School Musical

Soon after filming *The Derby Stallion*, Zac learned that he had won the role of Troy Bolton in *High School Musical*. Zac flew straight to Salt Lake City, Utah, in the USA, where the film would be made. For six hot summer weeks, Zac and the cast lived in the Little America Hotel. They rehearsed for two weeks before filming began. They practised for up to eight hours every day.

Zac and the cast rehearsed for weeks to perform numbers such as "Get'cha Head in the Game."

Practice makes perfect

In a mirror-lined studio, Zac learned complex dance
routines. He sang and danced while dribbling a basketball
for numbers like 'Get'cha Head in the Game'. Unlike many
cast members, Zac had no formal dance training. He had
grown up playing sports, and didn't know how to move his
body in the right way. Zac skipped breaks to cram in as
much practice as possible. He was often the last one to
get moves correct, but he always nailed it in the end. Zac's
dedication impressed the director, Kenny Ortega.

Director Kenny Ortega (far left) gave direction to Zac and Vanessa during filming.

"... you get to do cooler things; you get to be a more interesting person when you're playing someone else. You get to be all the things you wanted to be, or that you saw someone else be that was really cool ..."

Zac in an interview with The Guardian

On the set

Once rehearsals were over, filming began. Filmmakers shot *High School Musical* in 28 days at a real **high school** in Salt Lake City. Hundreds of film extras filled the set. Filming lasted for 14 to 16 hours every day.

After long days on set, Zac and the cast relaxed. They swam in the pool, ate in restaurants, and toured Salt Lake City. When the film **wrapped**, everyone was sad to go home. Zac had no idea that his little made-for-TV film was about to become a huge hit, and that the cast would soon be reunited.

high school a secondary school in the USA
wrap complete filming; a word used to signal the end of filming

A big debut

High School Musical **premiered** on the Disney Channel in January 2006. It became the most-watched Disney program ever made. Google searches for 'Zac Efron' numbered in their millions. Zac began appearing on the covers of teen magazines. At first he didn't think fame would change his life. Then he tried to go and see a film, and got mobbed by fans. He had to get used to his new superstar status. Despite his overnight success, Zac didn't forget his schoolwork. He graduated from Arroyo Grande High School in June 2006.

Back to school

High School Musical led to a best-selling album, a concert tour, an ice show, a series of books, a reality TV show, and two sequels. In *High School Musical 2* (2007), the cast work at a resort during the school holidays. Zac had to learn another new skill for the film – how to play golf. When *High School Musical 2* aired, 17.2 million fans tuned in. It became the most-watched cable TV program ever.

High School Musical 3: Senior Year (2008) follows the cast as they graduate, and attend their **high school** prom (a special ball for school leavers in the USA). It has even better dancing and catchier songs. Unlike the first two films, *High School Musical 3* was shown in cinemas. US fans spent £42 million on tickets in its opening weekend.

premiere the first public showing of a film

Hitting high notes

Zac did not sing all of Troy's songs in the first *High School Musical* film. His voice was blended with the singing voice of Drew Seeley, a Canadian actor and singer who wrote the hit song 'Get'cha Head in the Game'.

Zac did all his own singing in *High School Musical 2* and *3*, appearing on the smash hit soundtracks. He was even offered a record deal by Simon Cowell, but turned it down, saying that acting was his priority.

Zac and his co-stars attend the UK premiere of *High School Musical 3* in Leicester Square, London.

Hollywood calls

Zac's *High School Musical* success quickly led to other Hollywood roles. His singing and dancing skills were perfect for the film *Hairspray* (2007). Superstars Michelle Pfeiffer, Queen Latifah, and John Travolta also appeared in the musical. Zac played Link Larkin, the ultra-cool teen star of a hit dance show. To become Link, Zac cut his famous floppy hair and dyed it darker. He even put on 15 pounds (7 kilograms). *Hairspray* rehearsals lasted for two and a half months. The cast and crew filmed for another six months.

Hairspray **premiered** in London, Sydney, Australia, and three US cities (Los Angeles, Baltimore and New York). Zac hit the red carpet every time, and took to the dance floor at the Baltimore premiere to show off his moves! *Hairspray* was a big hit, and was nominated for Best Motion Picture (Musical or Comedy) at the 2008 Golden Globe Awards.

"In the 1960s, the clothes were very tight. I didn't want chicken legs."

Zac on why he gained weight for Hairspray, from an interview with Moviefone.

Excited fans greeted Zac at the Los Angeles premiere of Hairspray.

New challenges

Zac enjoyed making musicals, but he wanted to challenge himself by acting in different types of films. In *17 Again* (2009), he plays Mike, a man in his 30s who becomes trapped in a younger body, and gets to re-live his school days. Zac based his performance on his dad! His teenage fans made sure *17 Again* was a box office success.

Zac mixed teen-friendly roles with films that appeal to adults, such as *Me and Orson Welles* (2009). In this film, Zac plays Richard, an actor working with the famous director Orson Welles. The film is set in New York City in 1937. It was perfect for Zac, who loves the old films that Welles directed.

Next, Zac had a go at romance, playing the lead in *Charlie St. Cloud* (2010). This film is about a man who puts his life on hold after his brother dies. He surprises people by becoming a cemetery caretaker, but he has a good reason.

Zac and *Hairspray* co-star Nikki Blonsky became good friends.

Zac returned to romance in *The Lucky One* (2012), playing a marine who sets out to find a woman he has only ever seen in a photograph. He shocked his fans by shaving his hair for the role. Zac is also part of the superstar **ensemble cast** of *New Year's Eve* (2011). He was excited to film scenes with Michelle Pfeiffer again.

Hard work

Zac has a very strong work ethic. He takes time to learn more about the characters he plays. He respects directors and listens to their advice. He asks for extra takes to make sure his performances are perfect. Zac also works hard to promote his films. He often arrives early to interviews, and is polite and well-spoken.

Zac at the Oscars

Zac performed at the 2009 Academy Awards, also known as the Oscars. Millions watched as he sang and danced on stage with Beyonce, Hugh Jackman and his *High School Musical* co-star Vanessa. They performed a show-stopping extravaganza based on musicals. The following year, one of the Academy Awards producers asked his Twitter followers who they would like to see at the Oscars. The fans asked for more Zac! He was invited back to present awards in 2010 and 2011.

ensemble cast a cast where there is no lead performer. Each actor has an equally important role.

CHAPTER 5

Life in the spotlight

Since *High School Musical*, Zac's life has been filled with screaming fans and **paparazzi**. His schedule is packed with **auditions**, film shoots, interviews, and red-carpet events. There are even dolls that look like him. Despite his success, Zac insists he's still a normal guy. Instead of partying at celebrity hangouts, he enjoys spending time with his family and friends in Arroyo Grande. He now lives in Los Angeles, but misses his mum's cooking. When he's not working, Zac likes to stay active. He surfs, skis, snowboards, and skateboards. He also enjoys looking after two vintage cars that belonged to his grandfather.

Zac says that it's his fans that make him a star. When he is out in public, he is happy to sign autographs and pose for snapshots. But he also tries to keep his private life private. While he was dating his *High School Musical* co-star Vanessa, Zac did not talk about their relationship in interviews. He also avoids social networking websites.

paparazzi photographers who take unposed photos of celebrities

Zac spends his free time exercising, playing sports, and hanging out with family and friends.

Giving back

As soon as Zac became famous, he began donating time and money to charities. Zac's cousin and close friend Emily survived cancer, so Zac often raises money for healthcare charities, including the i2y Cancer Foundation. He has visited children's hospitals and schools, and has invited sick children to visit him on film sets. He also takes part in fundraising events that have required him to play golf, video games and even learn how to surf. Zac gets other people involved, too. On the set of *The Lucky One*, Zac convinced the cast and crew to cut their hair for charity.

Zac Efron helps out at a charity surf event in aid of the One Sight Foundation at Bondi Beach in Sydney, Australia.

Future plans

Zac is always on the lookout for new and exciting projects, from comedies to action thrillers. His fans can't wait to see what he does next. Zac's refusal to use social networking sites doesn't stop him being hot news on the Internet. Bloggers were the first to reveal that Zac's latest projects include several films for an adult audience. But he hasn't forgotten his younger fans. They will be able to enjoy his voiceover role in *The Lorax*, a 3D film of the Dr Seuss story about saving rainforests.

In 2010, Zac set up his own production company, called Ninjas Runnin' Wild. He is looking forward to working behind the camera and developing his own projects. These include the time-travel adventure *Einstein Theory* and *Fire*, where Zac will play a spy. He would also like to direct films one day. But for now, Zac says he just wants to "make great films, and be good in them".

Zac's awards

Zac has won dozens of awards for his films, personality and good looks! His first was Best Breakout Star at the 2006 Teen Choice Awards. More recently fans named him their Favourite Movie Star under 25 at the 2011 People's Choice Awards.

Glossary

agent someone who helps actors find work

audition a performance given by an actor when he or she is trying out for a part

autism a condition that causes people to have trouble communicating and forming relationships with others. Sufferers may have difficulty with language.

ensemble cast a cast where there is no lead performer. Each actor has an equally important role.

high school a secondary school in the USA

paparazzi photographers who take pictures of celebrities, and sell them to magazines or newspapers

premiere the first public showing of a film

project make your voice carry far

take the filming of a TV or film scene. Several takes may be needed to get the scene right.

wrap complete filming; a word used to signal the end of filming

Find out more

Books

10 Things You Need to Know About Being Famous, Jen Jones (Capstone Press, 2008)

Zac Efron, Christian Guiltenane (Michael Joseph, 2010)

Zac Efron A-Z, Alex Kincaid (John Blake, 2010)

High School Musical: The Essential Guide, Catherine Saunders (DK, 2008)

Websites

Get the latest Zac news, photos and gossip at his number one fansite:
www.zefron.com

Check out Zac in his most famous role, Troy Bolton, at the official High School Musical website:
tv.disney.go.com/disneychannel/originalmovies/highschoolmusical/

Find plots, photographs and quotes from Zac's latest film projects on his Internet Movie Database page:
www.imdb.com/name/nm1374980/

Index